Simple DIY Crafts for Fun & Decoration

Qasim .P Jordan

Simple DIY Crafts for Fun & Decoration : Creative and Easy DIY Ideas for Unique Handmade Decorations.

Introduction

This is a comprehensive guide that explores the art of quilling, providing history, instructions, and a variety of projects suitable for newcomers to this craft.

The guide begins with a look at the history of quilling, shedding light on the origins and evolution of this intricate paper art form. It sets the stage for what's to come and adds depth to your understanding of quilling.

Quilling materials and supplies are then introduced, ensuring that beginners have a grasp of the tools and items they'll need to embark on their quilling journey. This section helps you get organized and prepared for the projects ahead.

The guide truly shines with its detailed projects and instructions, making it a valuable resource for beginners. It starts with a festive "Quilled Christmas Tree" project that guides you through creating a beautiful paper tree using quilling techniques. The step-by-step instructions, accompanied by illustrations, make it accessible even for those with no prior experience.

"Quilled Christmas Cards" project takes your newfound quilling skills to the next level by teaching you how to craft stunning greeting cards with intricate designs. The guide ensures you have a head start on your holiday crafts.

"Quilled Snowflake Ornament" and "Star-Banner Ornament" projects extend your repertoire with delightful holiday-themed designs. The guide's detailed instructions empower you to produce eye-catching ornaments for your Christmas tree or to share as thoughtful gifts.

As Christmas comes around, the "Paper Ornaments Craft Project for Your Family Traditions Tree" and "Woodgrain Ornaments Craft Project for Your Family Traditions Tree" offer unique and personalized decoration ideas that can become cherished family heirlooms.

"Velvet Leaves Project for Your Christmas Tree" introduces a tactile element to your holiday decorations, bringing a touch of elegance and luxury to your quilled ornaments.

"Terrarium Ornaments" open up new possibilities for your quilling skills, showing you how to create mini paper gardens that can adorn your tree or be used as whimsical decor throughout the year.

The guide doesn't stop at personal creativity; it also delves into "Project Ideas to Make Money," offering insights into turning your quilling passion into a profitable venture. This section presents opportunities for selling your quilled creations and potentially building a small business from your craft.

In summary, this book is a well-structured and informative guide for those new to quilling. It combines history, supply knowledge, and a range of projects with clear instructions and illustrations to help beginners develop their quilling skills and explore the art form's creative possibilities. Whether you're interested in personal crafting or seeking to turn your hobby into a small business, this guide has something to offer.

Contents

CHAPTER 1: HISTORY

Quilling paper is a drawing of a piece of paper or a thin strip of paper made of different shapes and used to make the paper. This beautiful piece of paper is called a watermark/Filigree.

It is not surprising that this piece of art can be traced back to the 13th or 14th century in Europe, where quilling work was used to decorate religious objects.

Filigree handicrafts became popular in the eighteenth century, and quilling designs were used primarily in the development of other crafts, homewares, and furniture.

For centuries, quilling has been almost invisible to art. Although there are artists and painters around the world who keep this art form, few are aware of the design. In the past six years, paper quilling has gained popularity. This is necessary for the creation of different local groups and organizations that display publications and works of art using the material. Many print editions are now available online for printers. Free tips and quilling materials are also available online.

However, Paper quilling is easy to learn. The best thing is that you only need a few items to start this great craft activity. If you like making paper crafts and handicrafts, but have never quilled paper before, why not try? Who knows, one day you may be the creator of the best artistic quilling paper designs in the world.

CHAPTER TWO: QUILLING MATERIALS AND SUPPLIES

There are specific tools and materials for quilling paper. Some of the materials needed in this tutorial are:

BASIC QUILLING MATERIALS
- Quilling Paper

You can find strips of quilling paper at craft stores and also online at Amazon and more. They usually come in many different colors and are 3 to 5 mm wide.

- Quilling tool

This is usually available at craft stores, where you can find quilling paper. The quilling tool is used to wrap the paper strips on a coil. If you don't have a frilling tool, you can also use a toothpick, needle, or satay stick. The quilling tool can make quilling much easier if you are a beginner.

- Craft glue

Any PVA glue or clear glue for handmade paper can be used.

- Toothpick

You will need this to apply the glue to the quilling paper.

QUILLING MATERIALS IN DETAILS

1. Quilling Paper

Quilling paper crafts use strips of quilling paper that come in many different colors and dimensions. The weight of the quilling paper is between 80gsm and 100gsm. The width of each strip of paper varies from 1.5 to 10 cm.

2. Slotted tool

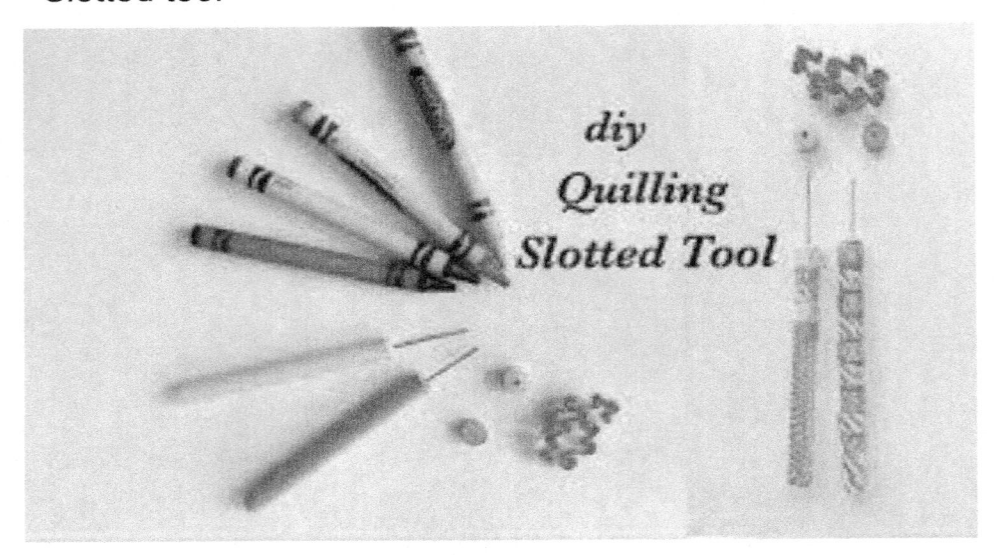

A slotted tool is used to wrap the strips of quilling paper on a coil. A toothpick can also be used to wrap the strip of paper, but the coil will have a larger hole in the center.

3. Craft glue

Any handmade glue can be used on the loose ends of the paper strips. Use the glue sparingly on the strips.

A toothpick can be used to apply the glue.

4. Quilling Board

When you want to create many coils of the same size, the quilling paper template plate is a great tool. The circle templates on the quilling board help to keep each coil in the correct size and measurement.

5. Paper Fringer

The paper indicator is used to make fringes on a strip of quill paper quickly. The fringe can also be made with scissors, but it takes time to do it, and sometimes the paper is not perfectly fringed. Fringed paper is used to make fringed flowers.

6.   Quilling Comb

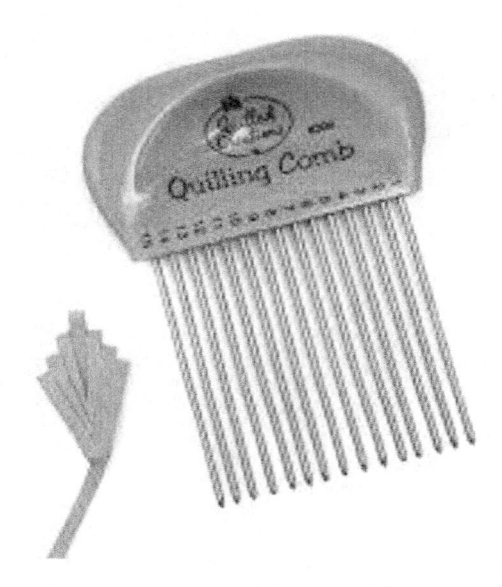

There are several techniques for making quilled paper crafts. One of the tools used for quilling is the quilling comb. A strip of paper is wrapped around the ends of the comb to make a quilled design.

7.   Scissors

Pointed scissors or a handmade knife is useful for fringing a strip of quilling paper and for trimming excess strips of quilling paper. Some people prefer to tear off the quilling paper when making quilled coils.

8. Crimper Tool

For making folded strips of quilling paper, a crimping tool is a useful tool. The quilling paper is inserted through the tool and folded by turning the handle.

9. Bulldog Clip

When making fringes manually with scissors, a bulldog clip is used as a guide when cutting. It can also be used to hold multiple strips for quilling paper, along with scissors.

QUILLING FESTIVITY PROJECTS! PROJECTS!! PROJECTS!!!

CHAPTER 3: PROJECT ON QUILLED CHRISTMAS TREE

This particular DIY project is a Beautiful DIY Quilled Christmas Tree. You will learn a-z on how to make on your own and when you are done crafting your quilled Christmas trees, you can use them to beautify your home or turn them into ornaments or probably glue them onto cards and give it out to family and friends as gifts.

SUPPLIES YOU NEED

- Paper quilling strips
- Green colored craft paper
- Slotted quilling tool

- Pencil
- Scissors

QUILLED STEPS

First, you need to select three different shades of green quilling strips for this craft. This will result in three layers of different colors. If you look at the photo of the finished product above, you will notice that there is some variation in the size of the quill strips. If you want to achieve this in your project, you can cut some strips 12 inches and others 6 inches.

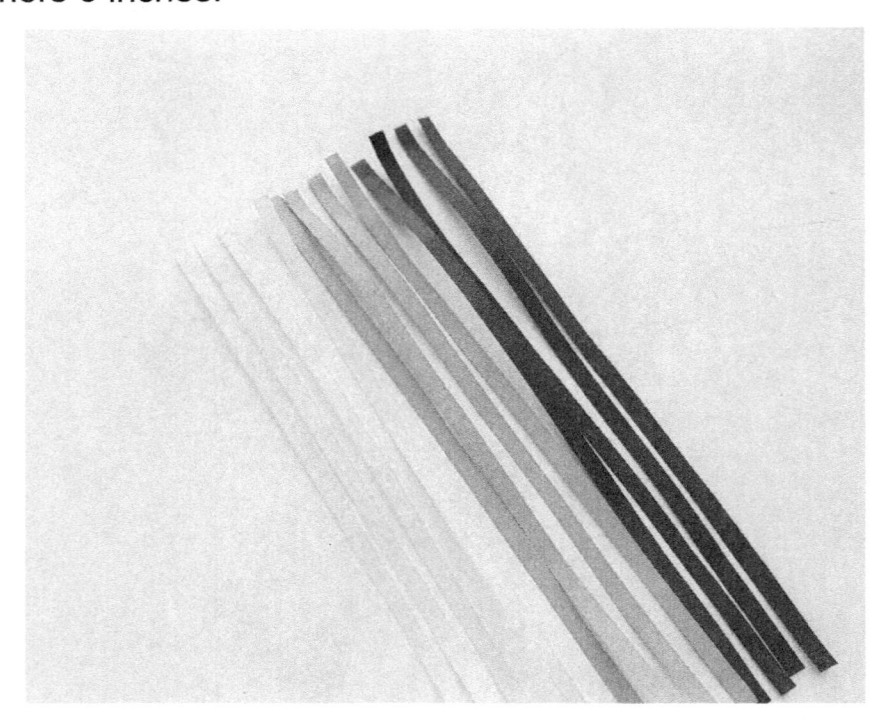

This next step is to pull out your quilling tool. Take a strip of any shades of green and wrap it tightly with the quilling tool. Carefully remove the spiral strip from the tool - it will look something like this. I will refer to this form simply as a "coil" as we go on.

Next, let's shape the coil into a "teardrop" look. To do this, let the coil loosen slightly, then squeeze the coil on one side to create a teardrop shape. Put a little glue on the open end of the strip to hold it firmly.

The third basic form that you need to know how to do is a "heart". To make a quilled heart, take a 30 cm long strip and fold it in half, as shown.

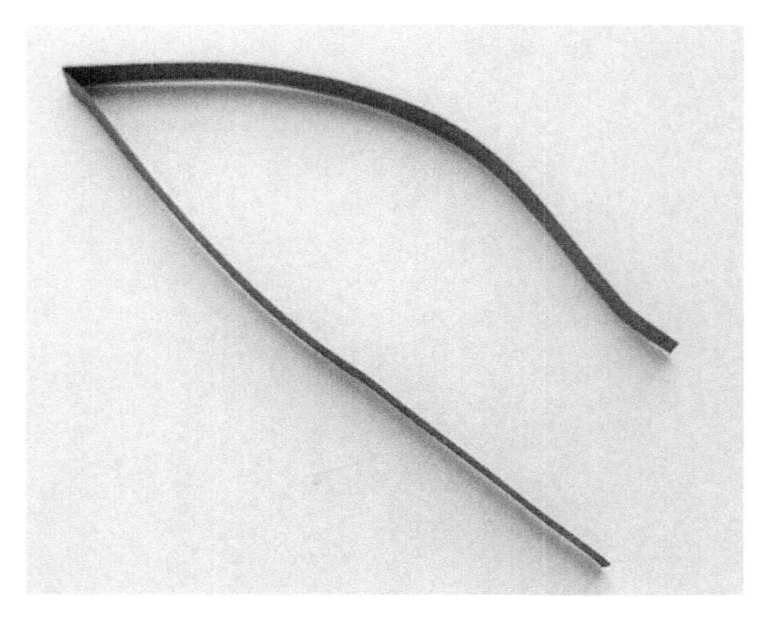

Use the quilling tool to wrap both sides of the folded strip, going inward to the curve in the middle. This will form a heart.

To make another shape look more complex, you can place the teardrop shape inside the heart shape between the 2 turns of the quilled heart shape. This creates a kind of triangle shape although very elaborate and decorative. If you look at the photo of the finished craft, you can see the shape you just created in several places in the design.

Now that you know how to make these basic shapes, you will use them to create some different feather designs that will be arranged on your Christmas tree. Don't worry about being exactly like the tree in our photo - yours will be original. However, here are some ways that will work well for your tree design. You have already practiced doing them in the steps above, so it will be easy!

- Coils

- Heart-shaped coils
- Teardrop-shaped coils
- Some heart shapes with teardrops inside
- A few teardrops shape with a coil attached

Now head-on with the steps and create a variation to pick from with all three shades of green!

After creating a large collection of quilled pieces in all shades of green, place them all in the same place, and take a green piece or craft paper. Now is when you can bring your own or your children's creativity. This will really please children who love Minecraft or Legos.

You want to start working at the top of the tree, first. For layers that go from top to bottom, I started with the lightest color at the top and the darkest at the bottom. Of course, you don't have to do this, but I think it looks good!

I found that three tear shapes worked perfectly for the top, "point" of the tree. If you want to do it this way, just arrange three drops on a tree-like tip and glue them to the handmade paper.

You are using the light green shade, arrange a few more quilled shapes under the three teardrop shapes to expand the top layer. When you are satisfied with the arrangement, stick each quilled strip in place.

You will use the same method to build your tree for the next two layers. For the middle layer, you can see that I used a heart shape with a tear in the middle, a teardrop on both sides, and two on the outside.

However, you do not need to use exactly those same forms. It is fun to build your own out of the dotted shapes you have created. Think of it as a creative challenge! Remember that you want to increase the width as you go down - you know, for that classic Christmas tree shape.

For the fourth layer, I used the darker green quilled shapes. Remember that you have the freedom to play with different arrangements and color variations before gluing anything. You can even mix the shades of green in each layer, or make more than four layers! Just have fun and be creative.

By now, you should be satisfied with your paper tree, it's time to add the finishing touches to bring out the extra beauty. The first thing you need is a star to the top! A five-pointed star is not difficult to make with a quilling tool and yellow stripes. You need to make five teardrop shapes and a regular bobbin for the center.

And then the tree needs something to support itself. Quill four loose coils using brown quilling strips. Arrange them in a square shape to form the tree trunk.

You may also want to wrap some small and tight bobbins to make ornaments for your tree! We chose red, but you can really use any color of your choice! For a beautifully decorated paper tree, slide the small coils into empty spaces on your tree but first put some glue on the outside. When everything is the way you want it, you can carefully cut out your design, leaving the green paper as the background.

You're done, and I'm sure your DIY quilled Christmas tree is beautiful!

If you make these beautiful DIY Quilled Christmas trees at home, you may want to tie a piece of string to one of the tears at the top so that you can hang it on your tree or probably that your kid can give out an ornament as a gift to a neighbor. You can also use the quilled tree to decorate a beautiful and season's greetings DIY craft card. There are many ways to use these beautiful paper trees to make your home even more festive this Christmas! Even more than that, I hope you enjoy the fun and memories it brings you while creating yours.

CHAPTER 4: PROJETC ON QUILLED CHRISTMAS CARDS

This chapter of this craft book will show you how to use paper quilling to create some beautiful Christmas Cards! If you follow the steps very well or use it as a guide to craft your own unique idea, I hope you get a lot of fun through making special memories with this craft.

I will walk you through how to make a beautiful Christmas card with a decorated Christmas tree. However, after learning how to craft beautiful images, you will probably be inspired to create your own unique Christmas card designs. While you're practicing by crafting your designs, it's advisable to try creating a few distinct shapes using your quilling tool and then planning out some Christmas designs using those shapes.

SUPPLIES NEEDED

- Paper quilling strips

- Colored craft paper
- Slotted quilling tool
- Pencil
- Scissors
- Craft Glue

QUILLED STEPS

For this Christmas tree card design, you will need 10 green quilling strips, 4 yellow quilling strips, and 1 brown quilling stripe. First, use your quilling tool to create 10 loose coils with the green strips. Use a little glue to protect the open ends. Your Christmas tree will be formed from these coils.

Then, create 4 loose coils with the yellow strips. Again, use a little glue to protect the open ends. Then, create a teardrop shape with them, joining each coil on one side, as shown below.

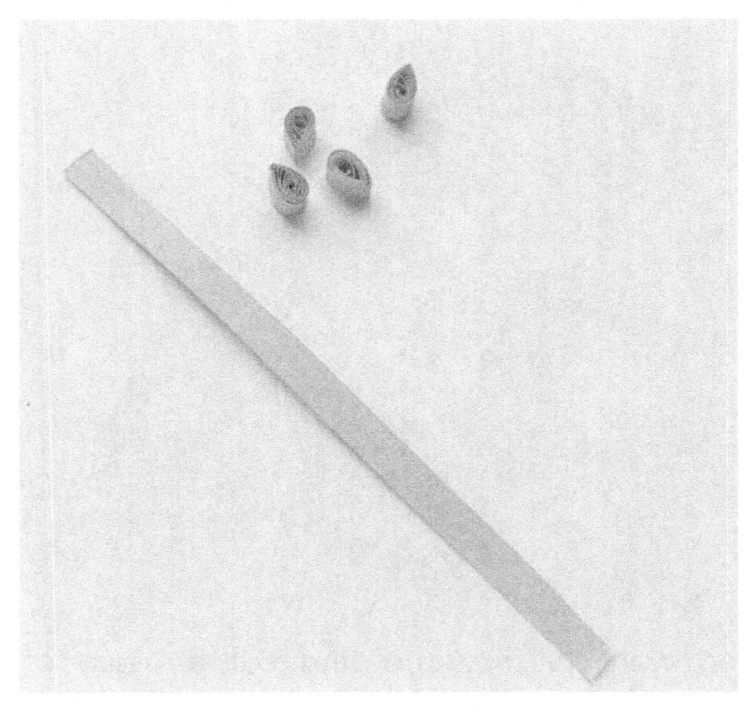

Finally, create a coil with the brown quilling strip and let it be very loose to an extent. Glue the open end, then create a square shape from the coil using your fingers. This is actually quite easy. All you need to do is press the flat shape in one of the directions. Let the shape open and then secure it in the other direction. This creates the effect of four equal sides (Square).

Now that you've finished making all the necessary shapes, it's time to put everything together for the design of your Christmas card. First, select a piece of cardboard or craft paper to make the card. Fold in half. If you would like to cut the paper so that your card is smaller, it is perfectly fine. Just make sure that the card will be slightly larger than the quilled design.

You will also want to measure and cut a piece of white craft paper/cardboard that is at least a few inches smaller than the card itself. This is the paper you will actually paste your design on, so play with it and make sure everything will fit the way you want it.

Let's start by organizing the tree. Take all the green coils you made and arrange them in a triangle shape, creating four lines. The bottom row will have four coils, the next row above will have three coils, the next row will contain two coils and a single to complete the top of your quilled Christmas tree! Just like as we have below.

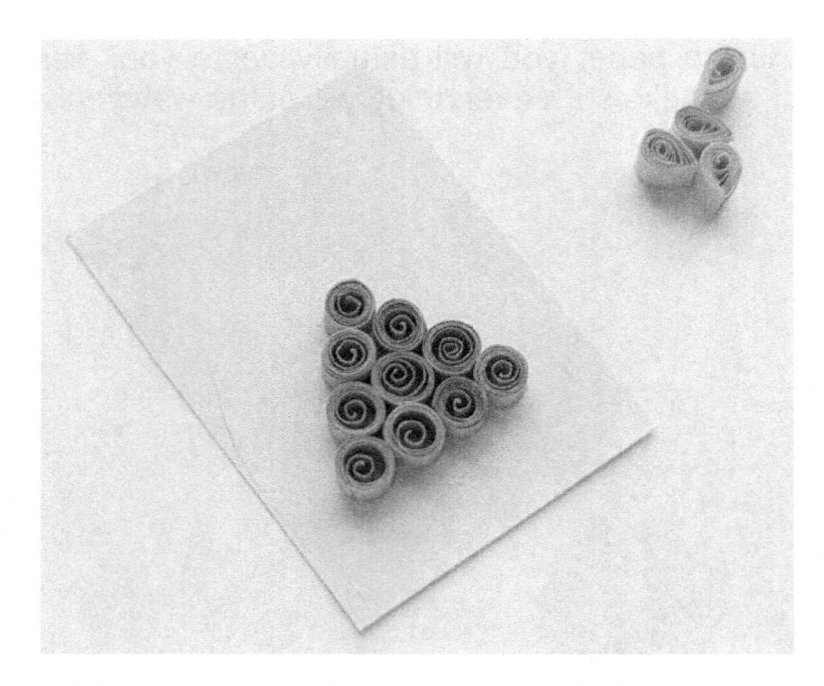

Next, you will create a beautiful star for the top of your tree using the yellow teardrop shapes. The four tips of the teardrops will create the four tips of your star.

Finally, take the brown square you created and glue it to form the trunk of your Christmas tree!

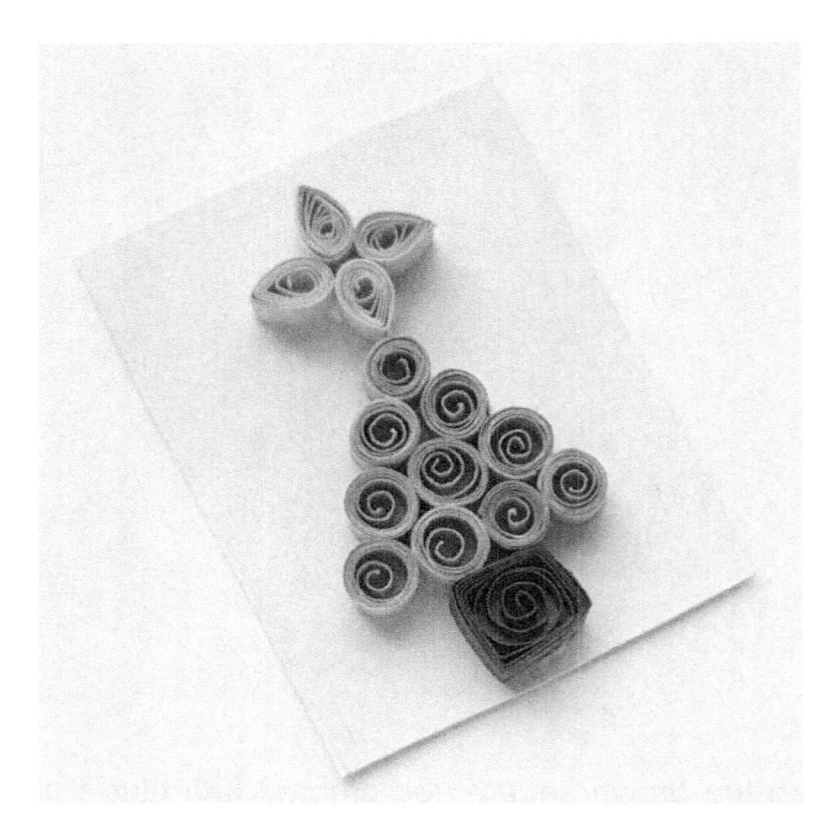

Now, all that remains is to paste the white piece of cardboard / handmade paper on the card, and you have a beautiful and carefully prepared Christmas card to donate.

Now that you have created this design, having fun thinking about other creative Christmas card designs that you can make with the shapes you just learned to make! If you're doing it as a family, it's going to be a lot of fun to see what everyone could craft.

CHAPTER 5: PROJECT ON QUILLED SNOWFLAKE ORNAMENT

Here in this chapter, I have great lessons to share with you on how to quilled Snowflakes ornament. Though it may look really difficult at first and detailed, it's not that had to craft. Trust me as I walk you throughout the process engagingly and easily.

I have crafted a lot of them over the years and they never fail to inspire oohs and aahs. This is a perfect application for quilling especially when festivity is in the air. Snowflakes are best when they are all twisted and rolled, and that's where quilling is at its most enjoyable too. You just need to remember that it's just rolled paper and dividing it into each little piece.

Cut a bunch of 1/4 " strips from a 12 x 12 piece of cardstock. I like to use an ice blue color, but a real white looks good too. You can make your strips thicker if you want and it will work just fine. They will look a little more substantial against the tree or in a package and will be a little more repellent. I happen to like the lacy appearance of the thinner strips and I think they are tough enough.

QUILLED STEPS

Cut out these measurements from the thin strips.

STRIPS CUTS

1 – 6" for the center round

8 – 3" for the arms

4 – 6" for the scrolls

4 – 3" for the teardrop

4 – 2" for the marquis

You will need some sort of quilling tool, which can be found in one of the chapters already discussed above. Or you can simply improvise your own by cutting the tip of a needle with cutting pliers or cutter or preferably a toothpick can serve.

Insert the strip of paper into the groove of the quilling tool, bring the tool to the end of the paper, and start to roll.

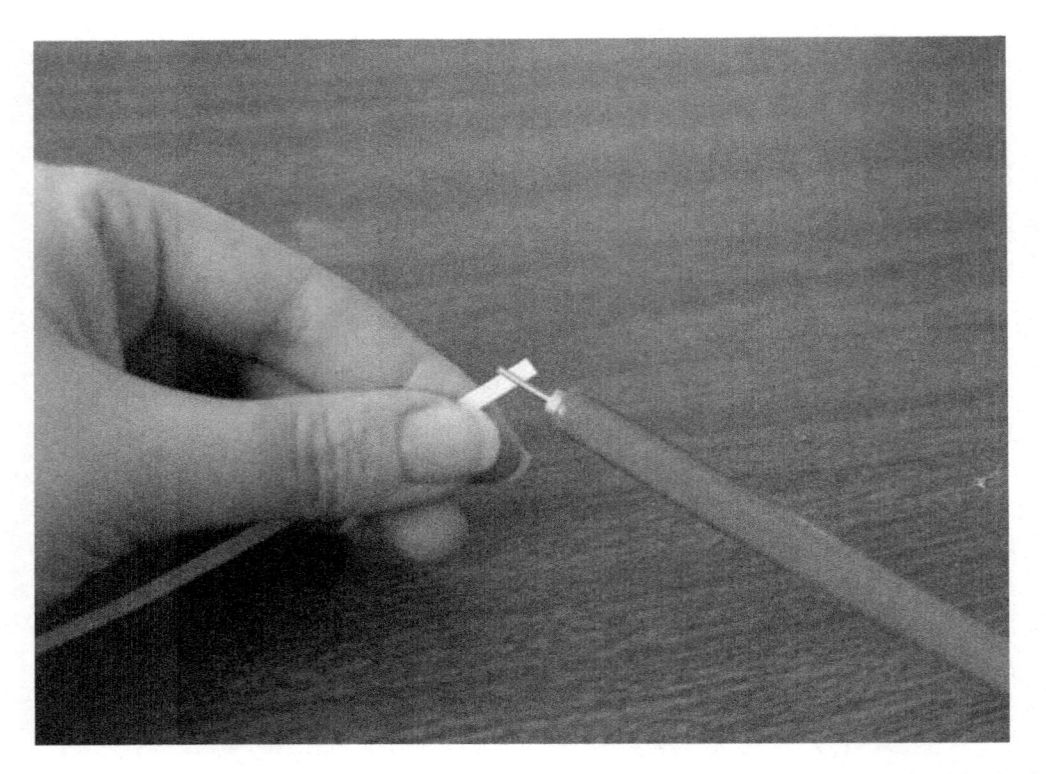

Let's start with the central 6 " round. Once you have mastered the round shape, you can do any other shape. And it's even easier than it looks. Roll it up completely and then let it go so that it relaxes in a looser circle.

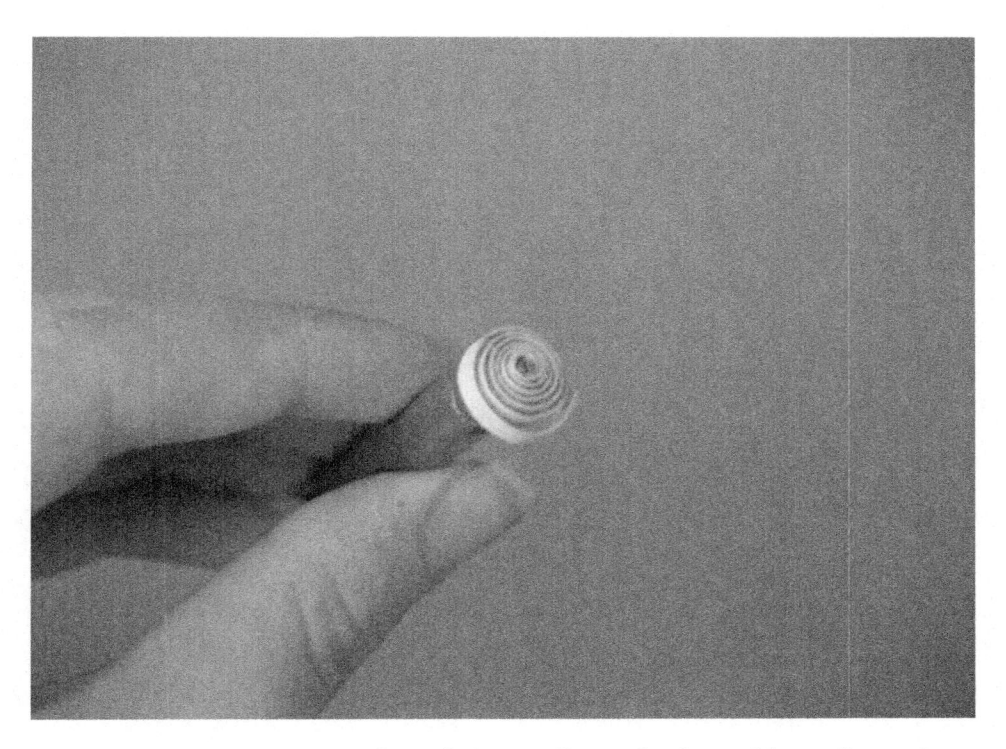

Apply a little glue on the tip of the tail and glue. Usually, when you feather, you tear the end off before gluing the other end. This torn feathered edge mixes with the rest of the shape, where a cut end will form a definitive crest. Here, you won't notice any crests, so there's no point in taking an extra step.

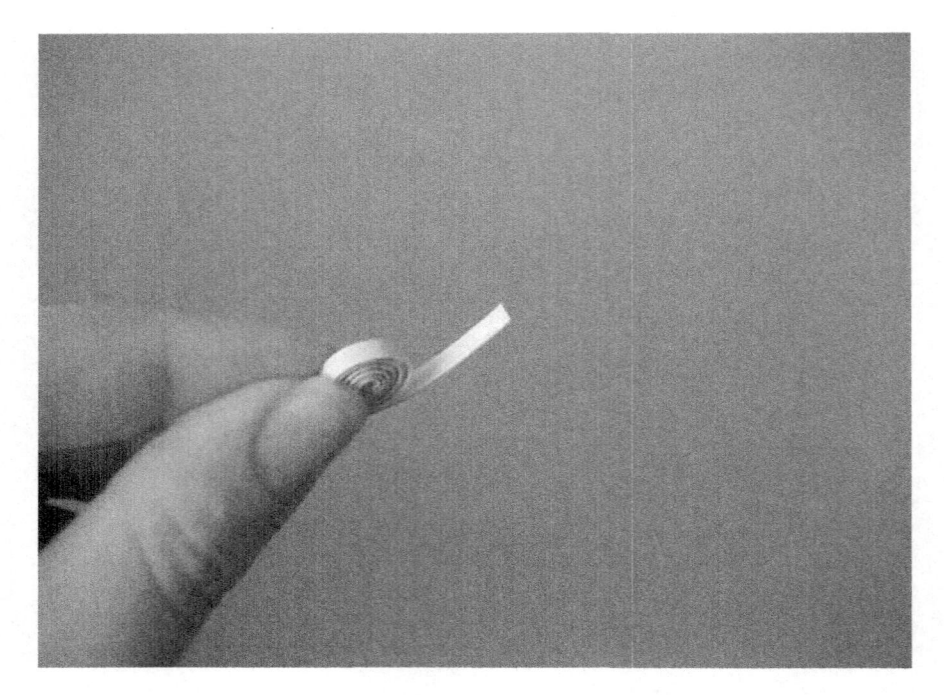

The round shape also provides a base for the teardrop and the marquis.

For the teardrop shape, you will take one side of a round made from one of the 3 ″ strips and pinch to create a point. Since we are not concerned with mixing our tips, I try to align this crest with the tip at the top of the tear to disguise it.

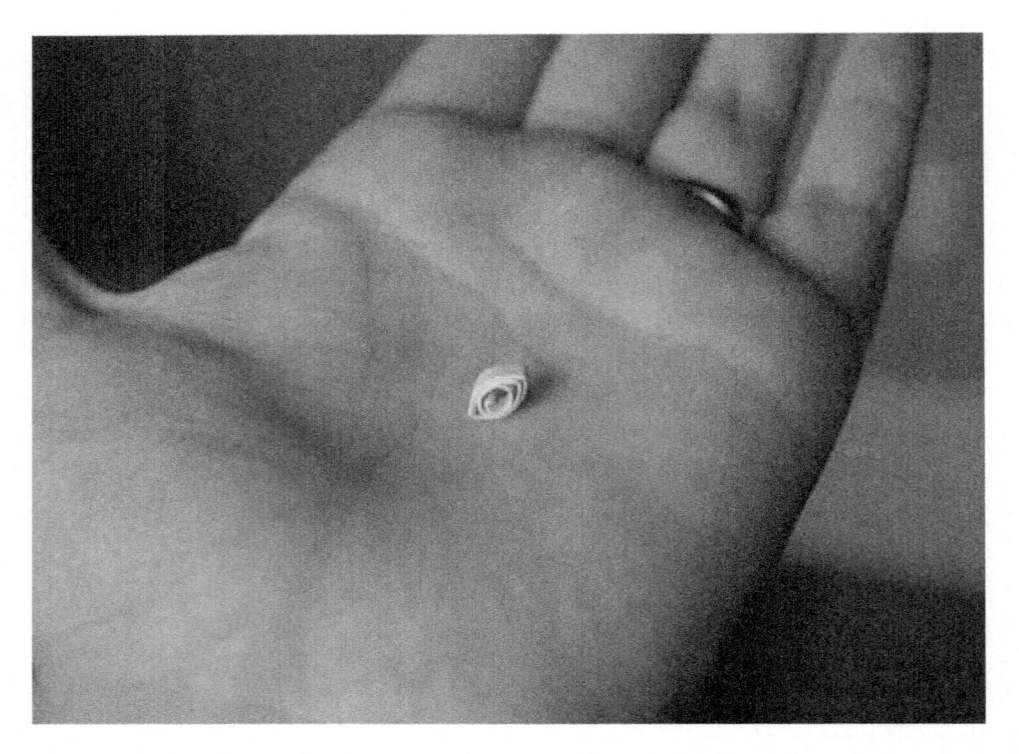

The marquis is done in the same way. Round off with a 2 " strip, glue the end in place and pinch both ends to create two ends.

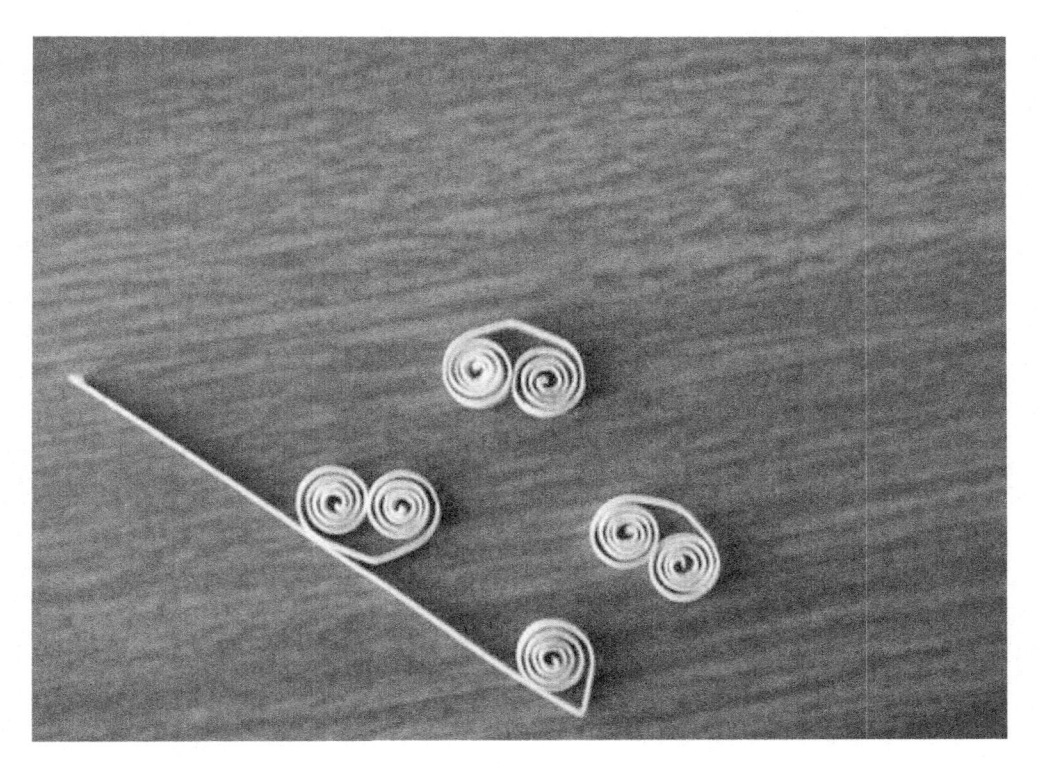

Next, let's make the scrolls by rolling a 6 " strip in half and curl every end halfway. As it is, this is a heart shape. Normally, a scroll is not folded, but it helps to have a measurement point and we are going to paste that point anyway, so it will not appear.

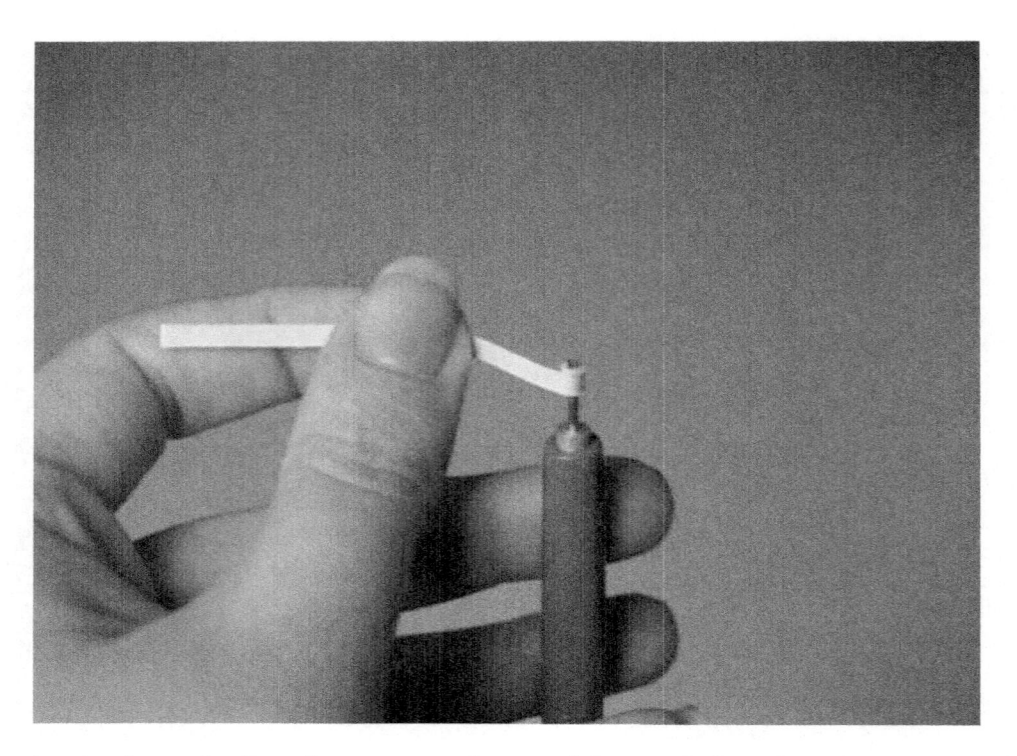

The last piece is for the arms, formed by a 3 ″ strip. At one end of the strip, wrap about two times.

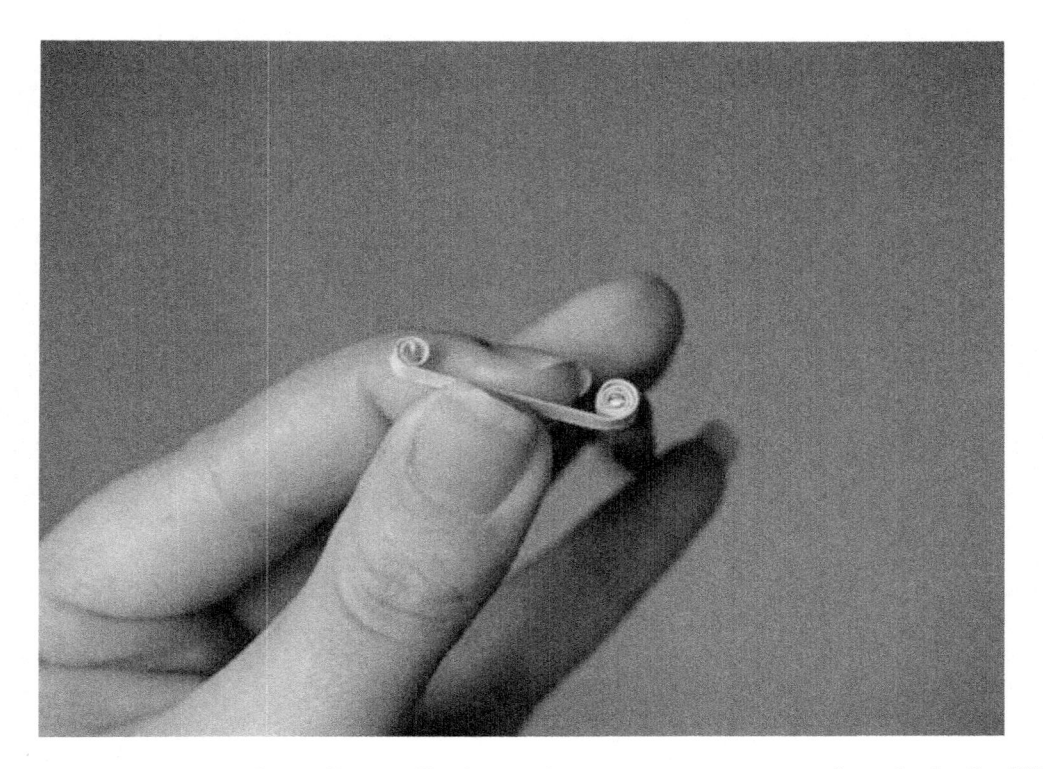

At the other end, roll until the piece measures about 1 ″. The measurements are loose here. The only thing that matters is that they are almost the same height. It doesn't matter if that height is a fraction of an inch taller or shorter.

That's it. You did all your pieces. The remaining crafting process is putting it all together. Start by taking 2 of the arms and gluing them back to back. With this step complete, you should have:

1 round

4 teardrops

4 marquis

4 scrolls

4 arm pieces

Start with the round piece. This will be the center. Then there are the arm pieces. Tap the edges of these bottom ties side by side and glue each piece to the round.

Now take a scroll and stick it on the small loops you hit.

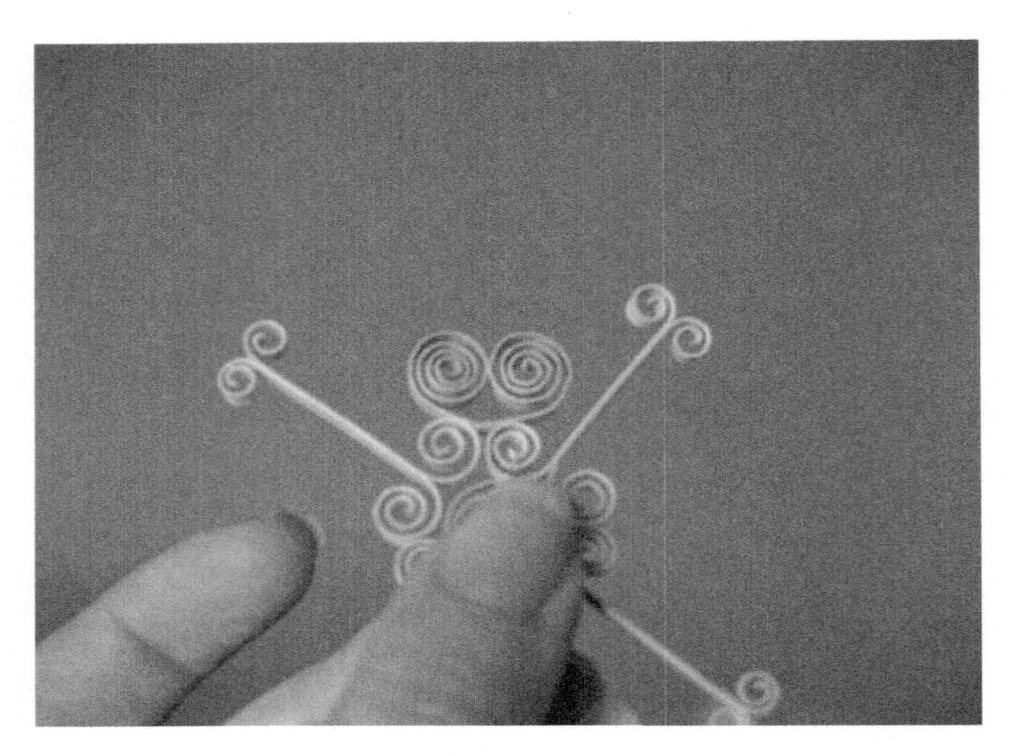

Carefully pull the roller out until it touches the arms and sticks them where they are.

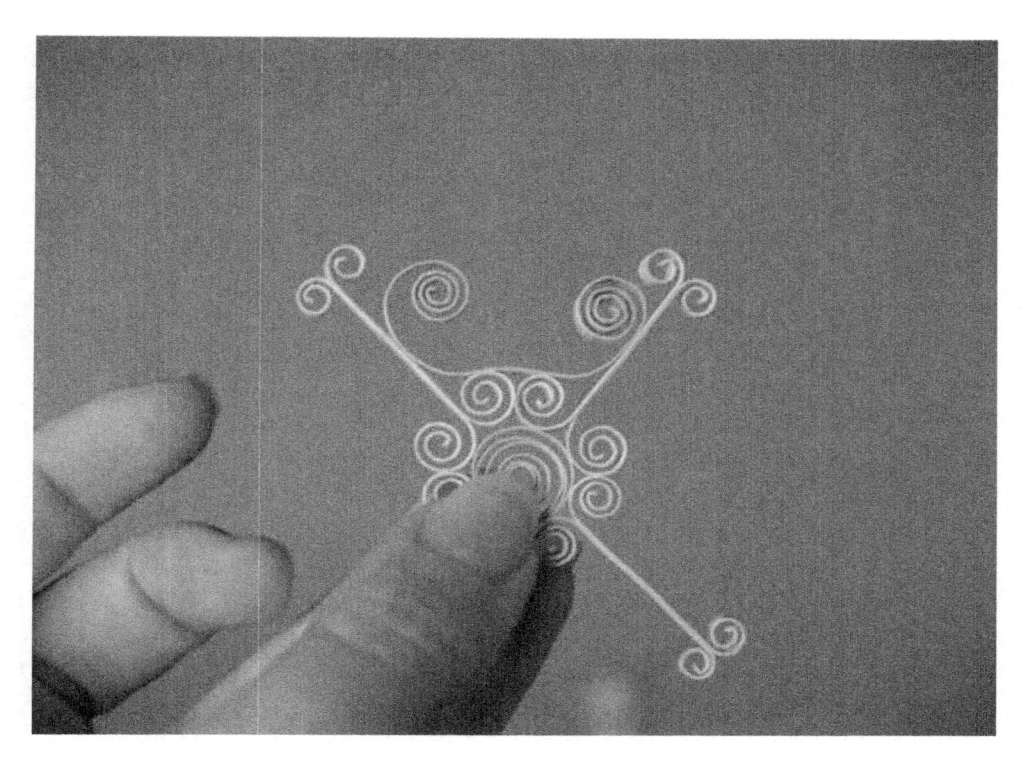

Take one of your tears and stick it in the middle of the parchment. Then, pull the rollers to find the tear and stick. Don't be afraid to unveil the scroll as much as you need. If your arm is bending or you don't want to stick to the tear, you just need to give it a little more space.

Repeat these steps for all sides and then paste the marquis in the small space between the straps on the upper arms.

For the snowflakes on my tree, I sprayed the finished snowflake with a spray adhesive and dipped it in glitter. I tried a liquid glue first, but I tended to make all the loops unfold. Then I put a loop of fishing line on one of the marquis to hang the ornament. I liked the idea of using the fishing line to make it look like the snowflakes were falling instead of hanging.

This could not be cheaper. You can get almost 10 ornaments from a sheet of paper, and they are incredibly easy to make in large batches. Last year, I had to make ornaments for 35 teenagers, and these were the ones I looked for. Ultimate budget savings, yet super sophisticated.

CHAPTER 6: PROJECT ON STAR-BANNER ORNAMENT

In this chapter, I will walk you through how you can craft your star banner ornament which will serve as a great fit for your Christmas tree. Nothing I do is complete without a little text, and there are so many good texts to choose from in the story of the crib. I wanted to make an ornament that incorporated part of the joy of the scriptures. I think the finished ornament is something that anyone could use, with the words that would make you felicitous.

These papier-mache star ornaments can probably be found or have something similar at your favorite craft store. I chose not to coat the edges with paper, so I opted for a quick finish of blue paint.

Cover one side of the ornament with mod podge and paste on the wrong side of a large piece of scrapbook paper. Normally you decouple the two sides of the paper to prevent it from bubbling, but I didn't want a decoupage appearance for the ornament, so I just let the ornament dry under something heavy so that the paper was flat.

When it is dry, cut the paper in line with the sides of the ornament and repeat the process for the back.

Cover the raw edges with a thin line of glue and sprinkle glitter on top. Shake off the excess.

Print your word on cardboard and cut it out. Make notches on the ends to make it look more like a banner.

Apply sparkle to the edges just like you did on the ornament.

To give the banner some dimension and make it look like it is unfolding, place two dots of hot glue at the beginning and end of the word, then glue it to the star ornament while putting the ends together.

I love the look of this ornament so much that I think I'll end up using this idea again in different ways. I can already see a home for them on my family's traditional Christmas tree with our family's name on the banner. This can also be a very simple and fun gift to personalize for teachers or neighbors. Wherever you want to include a few words, do it in a way that you sing.

CHAPTER 7: PAPER ORNAMENTS CRAFT PROJECT FOR YOUR FAMILY TRADITIONS TREE

This chapter will guide you through how you can craft your lovely paper ornaments while at the back of my mind, I have wanted to remake this tree for years. But the first practice batch of ornaments took me a long time, and I always had some other goal that needed attention, so, year after year, it was neglected.

This year I knew it was time to fix this especially as the world is coping with the Covid-19 pandemic, so I had to come up with some extra cheap and quick decorations. I bought a scrapbook paper package made by American Crafts who I love. They are a great company with beautiful unique designs. And I searched the internet for all kinds of paper ornaments I could find.

This is all very easy. And you can't get cheaper than paper, so they're perfect for a "disposable" application, like changing a color scheme year by year, or, like my friend who's getting married on December 19, decorating a winter wedding.

The globe ornament is old, but tasty, that I saw everywhere, from Carol Duvall to Martha Stewart and on a million different sites on the Internet.

The ornament made of strips of paper is quite instinctive. In fact, as I've been checking various DIY sites, I came across these exact embellishments, in exactly the same American Craft paper package. But sorry, I can't remember who it was, but I had a lot of fun watching it. I just cut a ton of strips of paper into a random size that felt good, drilled holes at both ends, and fastened them with nails. I made sure to make the interior beautiful, too, so I lined up the strips of paper with the opposite sides before placing the brads.

The heart is the only paper ornament that can claim some originality.

Cut four strips of 12 ″ by 1 1/2 ″ paper and four strips of 8 ″ by 1 1/2 ″ paper. I think it looks better when you use four different papers, so you end up with different patterns on each surface of the heart. But for this learning process, we are going with only two.

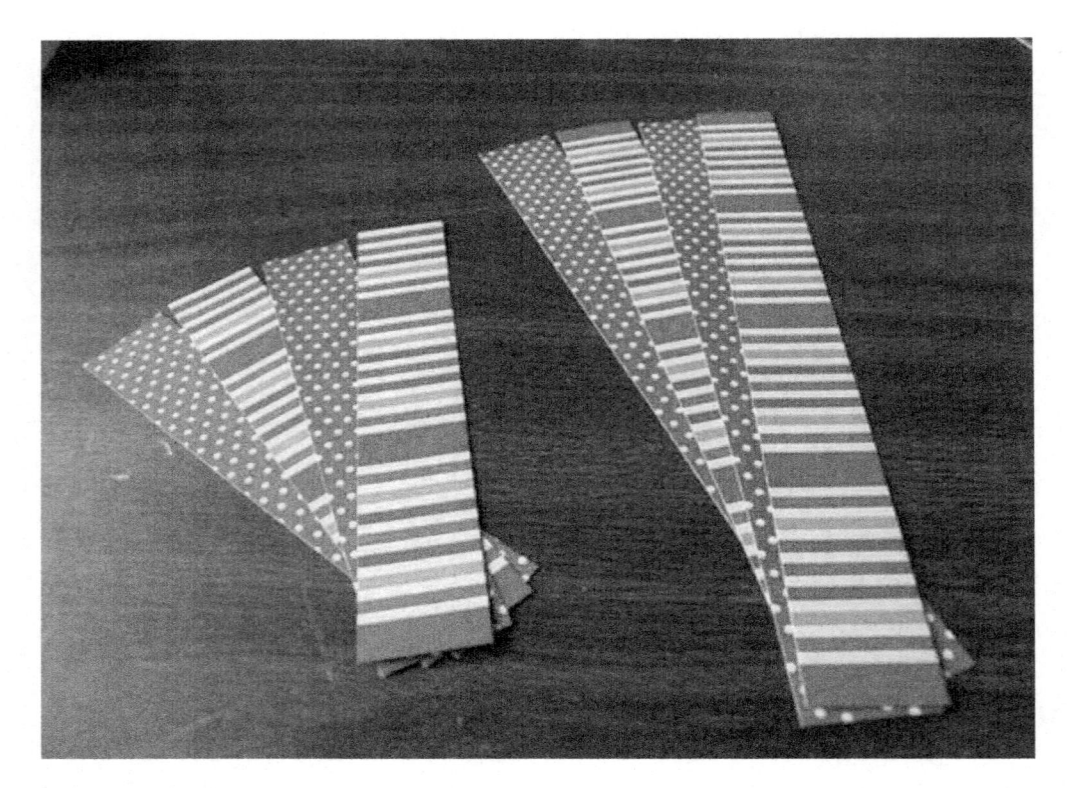

Glue two strips of 12 " back to back, the other two strips of 12 " back to back, and then the two sets of 8 " strips back to back, so that you have four double-sided strips with patterns different on both sides.

Align all four strips to be uniform on one side. You should arrange them so that when you fold them in the next step, the patterns are all in place. Place the 12 "strips on the right side together (and on the right sides I mean the side you want facing out of the heart), then place an 8" strip on each side with the right side of the 8 "strip facing the wrong side of the 12 "Strip. This is one of those things that is kind of hard to explain, but ridiculously easy in practice. You'll see what I'm talking about once you have the strips in your hands.

Fold the top end of each strip to find the bottom end, where you have everything aligned. Watch? There is your heart. If any of the strips are facing the wrong way, now is your chance to fix them.

Tighten the end with a few clips. I covered the clip with another small strip of paper, but you can also use tape, or just a nice clip and leave it exposed.

I used a little glue to attach a hanger between the curves of the heart. It also had the added benefit of making the heart a little more resilient.

CHAPTER 8: WOODGRAIN ORNAMENTS CRAFT PROJECT FOR YOUR FAMILY TRADITIONS TREE

I knew I needed to use wood in some way, but I don't have the cool power tools - just the boring ones, so I turned to the art of marquetry. It's something I never did, but I admire it a long time ago, so I bought a bunch of different types of wood veneers and started cutting things into animal shapes, but every time I tried to turn a corner, I started right along the grain. I think I have a lot to learn about marquetry.

I took the circle cutters I use in the scrapbook and decided to keep things easy for me.

For each ornament, cut 2 large oval shapes from wood and 1 large oval from cardboard. Glue these pieces together with the cardboard in the middle and let it dry with something heavy on top. The wood will be warped like paper when it gets wet, so make sure it dries well.

Cut a bunch of ovals in various sizes, from a bunch of different woods. Contrast is very important here, so make sure your woods are not too similar in tone.

Then, just combine ovals of different sizes in different wood tones until you get an image you like. I liked to let some oval shapes come out of the edge and then cut them off when the glue had dried. Place something heavy on it and let it dry and alternate both sides.

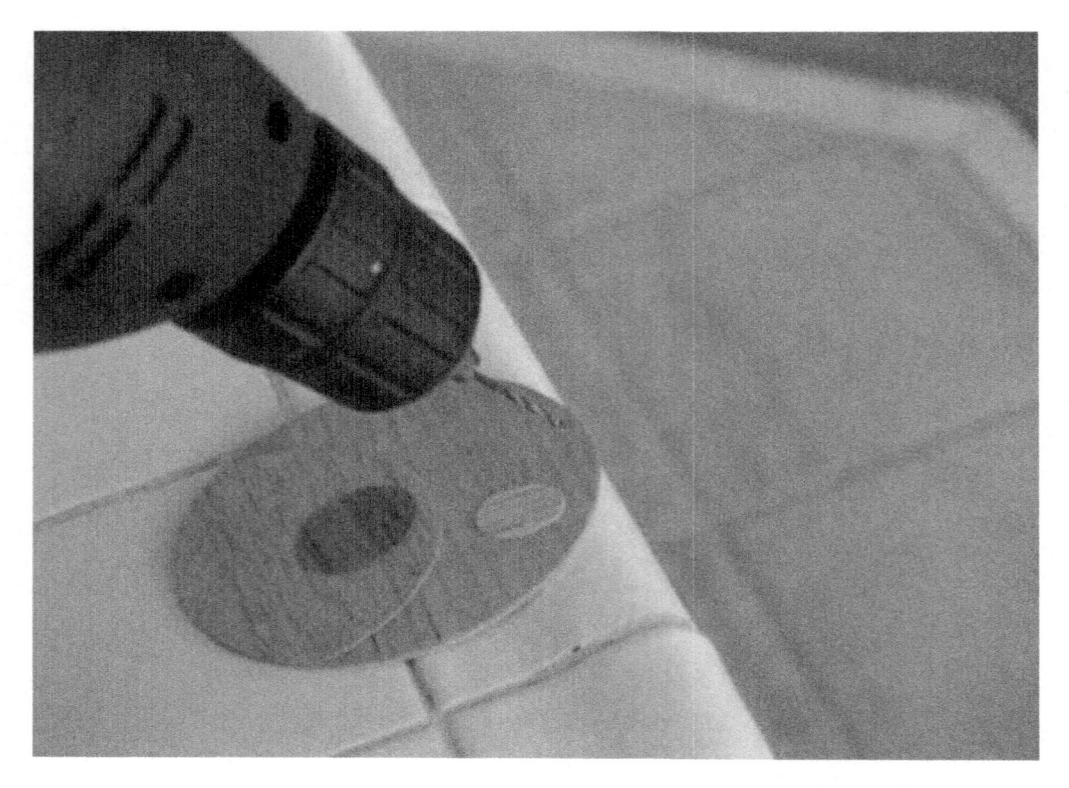

Use a small drill to make a hole for hanging and then thread a piece of ribbon or fishing line.

It took me many failed attempts and pieces of wood, but I think I made it in the end. It brings that amazing wooden look to my forest tree, but I don't think it's so modern as to look out of place with everything else.

CHAPTER 9: VELVET LEAVES PROJECT FOR YOUR CHRISTMAS TREE

This chapter will teach you how to make a simple and easy Velvet leaves designs for your festivity celebration. This project is inspired by Carol Duvall's fashion show and all the embossed velvet designs that she presents, I made this garland consisting of a zillion sheets of embossed velvet that I pasted on a wire and braided. When I thought about what would be in a tree in the forest, I knew I would have to revisit this project.

Begin by cutting two pieces for each Velvet you want to make. I folded the opposite side of my fabric and cut both at the same time to get as close as possible to an exact match.

Pass a drop of hot glue in the center and place a piece of floral wire on it. Watch out for those fingers!

Apply a little hot glue around the side of the leave shape Velvet and place the other piece of the cutout design on top.

To stop any velvet spills I may want, avoid any type of hem and add another opportunity for my beloved glitter, I ran a line of fabric paint around the outer edge of the leave. I know you probably hear fabric paint and shudder at the thought of bloated look, but if you apply a thin layer, all you'll see is glitter and it will still answer all other problems.

To put them on the tree, I arranged a few and then twisted their wires around a tree branch. For a garland, I just braided the strands. You can make your creative ideas from this by cutting your velvet shape to your favorite leaves and probably using a mixed color.

CHAPTER 10: WISE MEN CHRISTMAS ORNAMENT MADE WITH CLAY

The only craft teacher I ever had was Carol Duvall, on HGTV's glory days, when she showed something other than room renovations. She introduced me to the techniques of stamping, craft on papermaking, and, strangest to me, polymer clay. Following her example, I have experimented a little over the years and now I am a huge fan. Polymer clay is easy to work with, incredibly indulgent, and can bake in your home oven without any special firing. The colors are so vibrant that I knew it would be perfect for crafting three wise men and looks amazing when hanging on your Christmas tree.

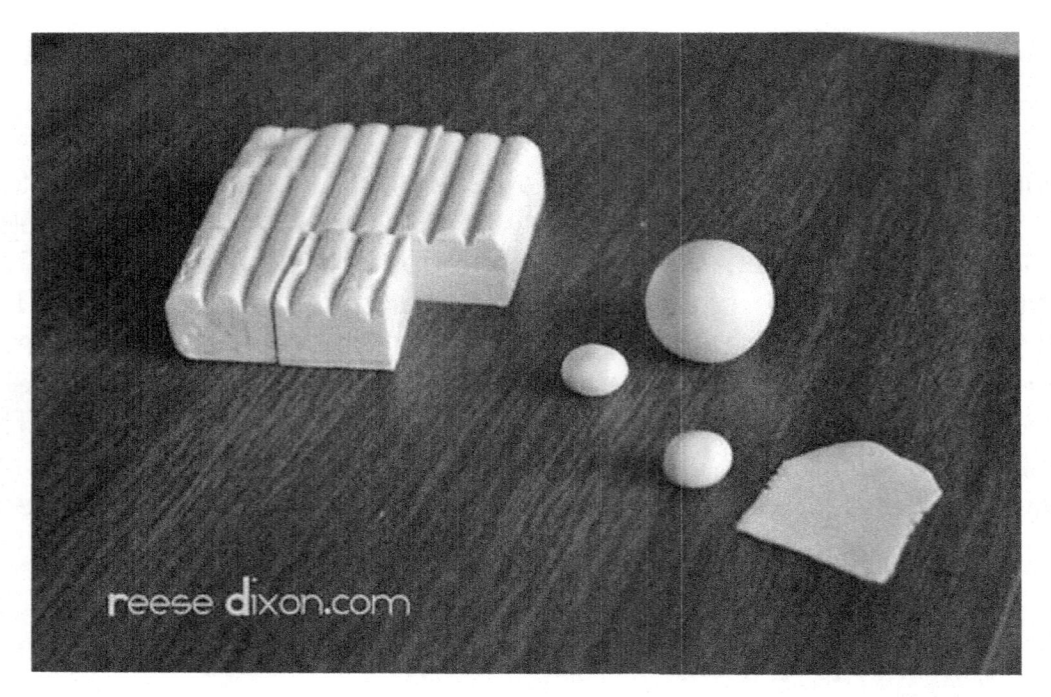

I prefer not to use a specific measurement for this project, especially when molding images of people. The different heights and shaped heads only add to the charm of things. But, roughly speaking, I took a brick of peach clay, cut it into 9 equal portions, and divided that small piece to make a round head and three balls. Two of these balls will be for the hands, and then roll the third to make the neck.

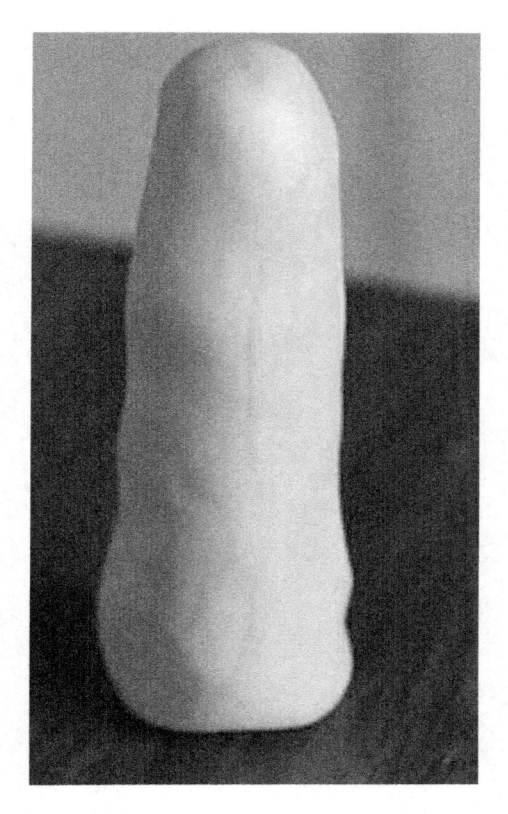

Make the body by wrapping clay in a cone about 7 centimeters high, more or less. I like to use clay remnants for this piece, which is leftover from an old project because everything will be covered. If you make the cone in some kind of flesh color, you can avoid the neck covering step.

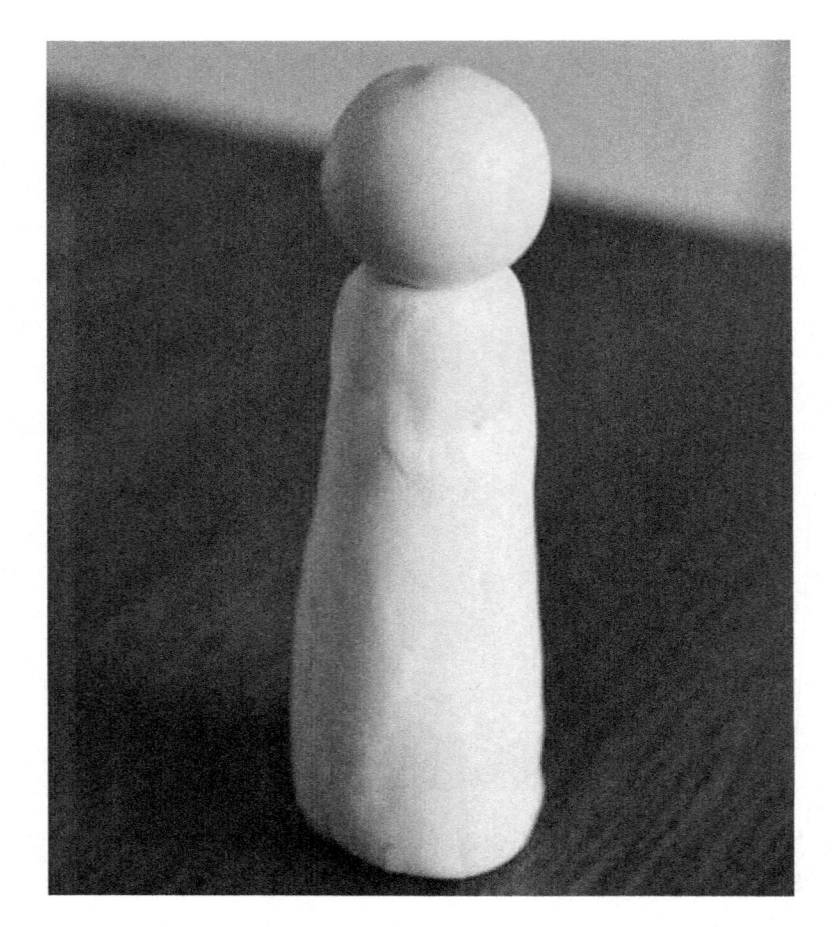

Cover the top of the cone with the flat peach square and glue the head over it. You can work the clay manually and roll it with any type of roller, but if you take a small rolling pin available where you buy the clay, you will be able to get that superfine flat square.

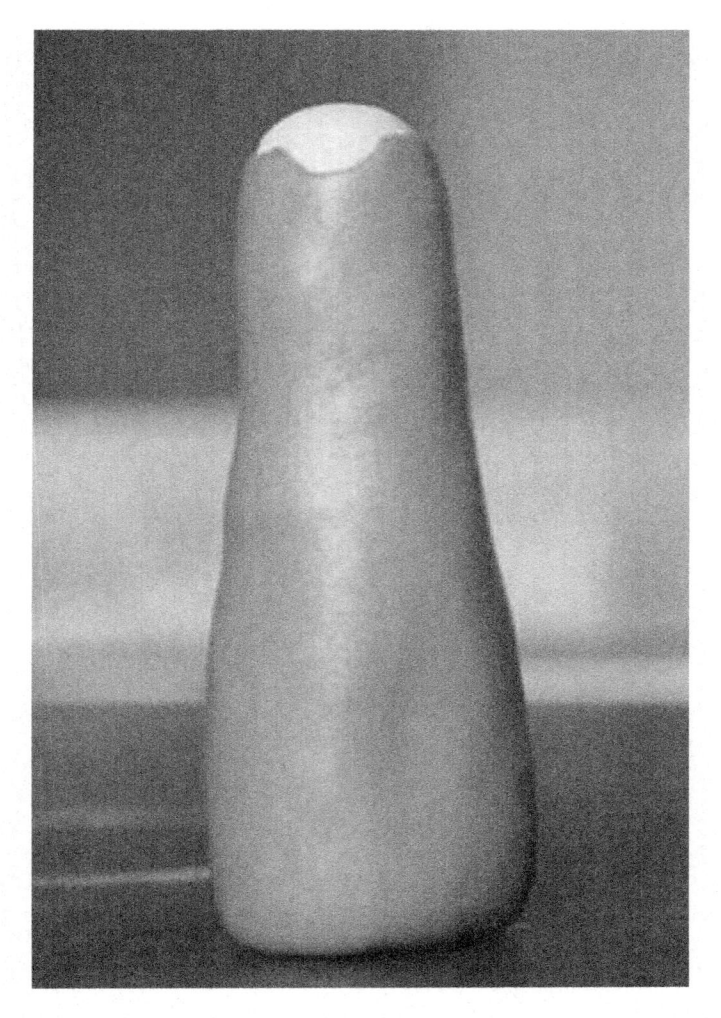

Open a square of clay until it is large enough to wrap around the cone and cover the bottom. Trim any uneven edges for a clean neckline and cut a U-shape in the middle of the top edge to create a round neckline. Blend the edges to create a smooth tunic.

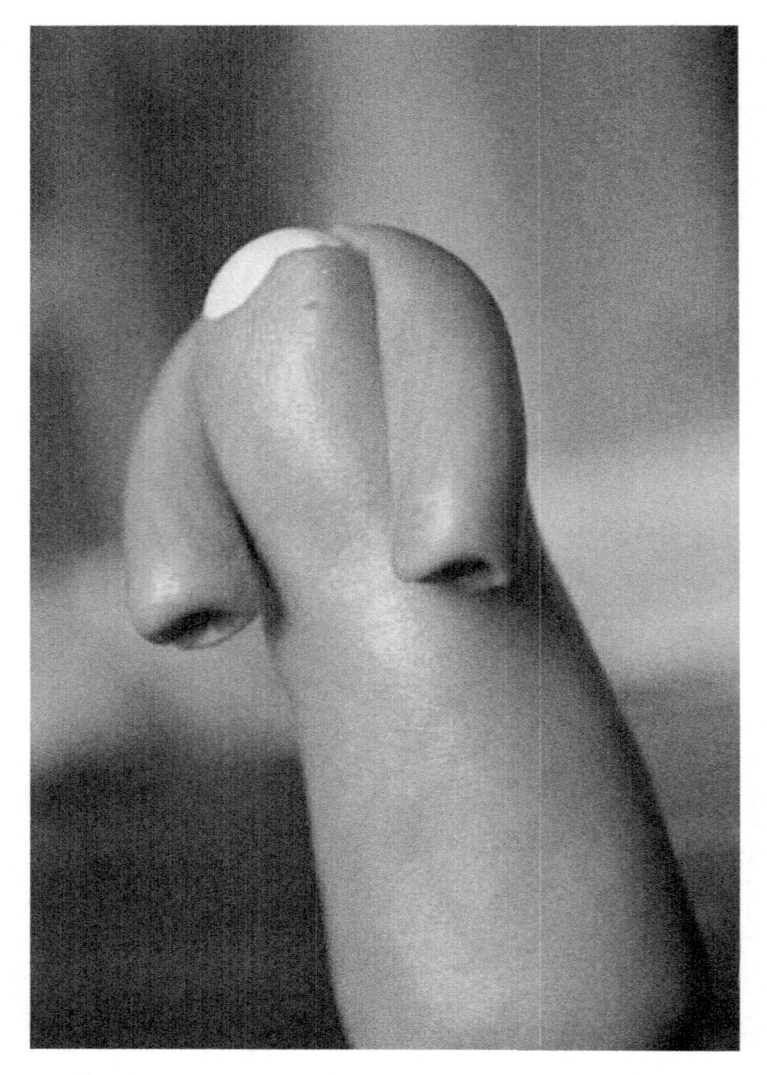

Wrap two snakes the same color as your tunic, about an inch long. Press the tip of a brush on one end of each sleeve to make room for your hand. Attach your arms to the top of your body and blend.

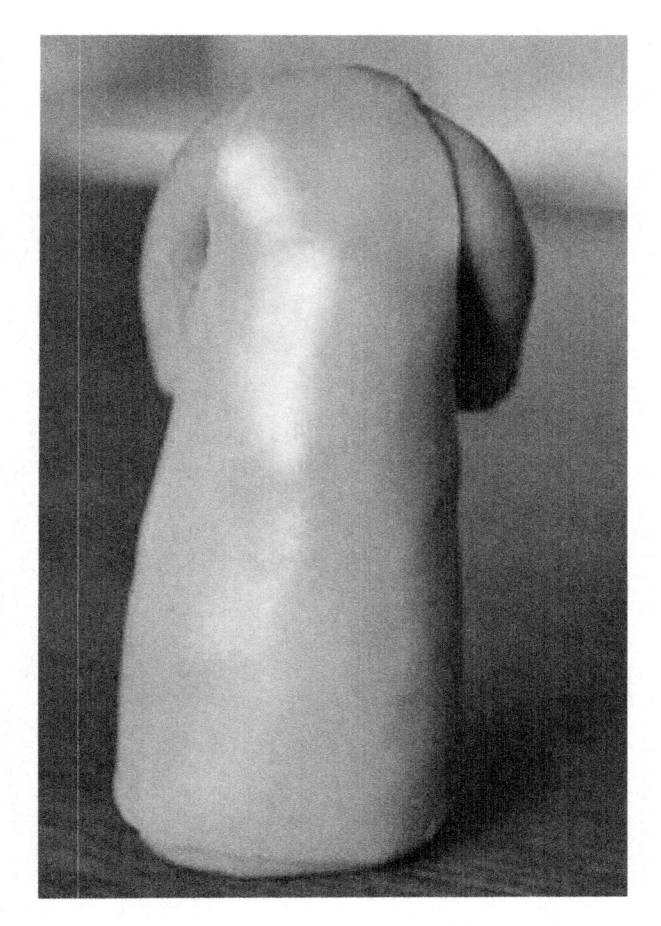

To make the vest, unroll an olive green square large enough to cover the back, trimming the edges with a razor blade or exact knife to create a smooth hem.

Roll another square and cut it in half to make the front of the vest. Join the front to the back on the shoulders and gently mix the seam.

Roll a small brown ball to make a belt, leaving the edges messy.

Press the small peach balls into space we made in the sleeves. Wrap a long, thin clay snake and wrap it around your head to make a turban. To make the face, add a small ball for the nose, small black beads for the eyes, then use a toothpick or the back of an exact blade to mark some wrinkles around each eye and a smile to the mouth.

Create a presentation for the wise man to take along to the manger by pinching some clay into an unpolished square and adding a golden handle.

After learning the basics, you can modify the features to make them look different. This sage has a beard, some hair, and a crown, around package instead of a square one, and a jacket instead of a vest.

This wise man wears only an ornate tunic and scarf, with a gift bag.

Once all of your wise are ready, poke a hole piece through the shoulders with a medium gauge wire. Then bake by following the instructions on the clay packaging.

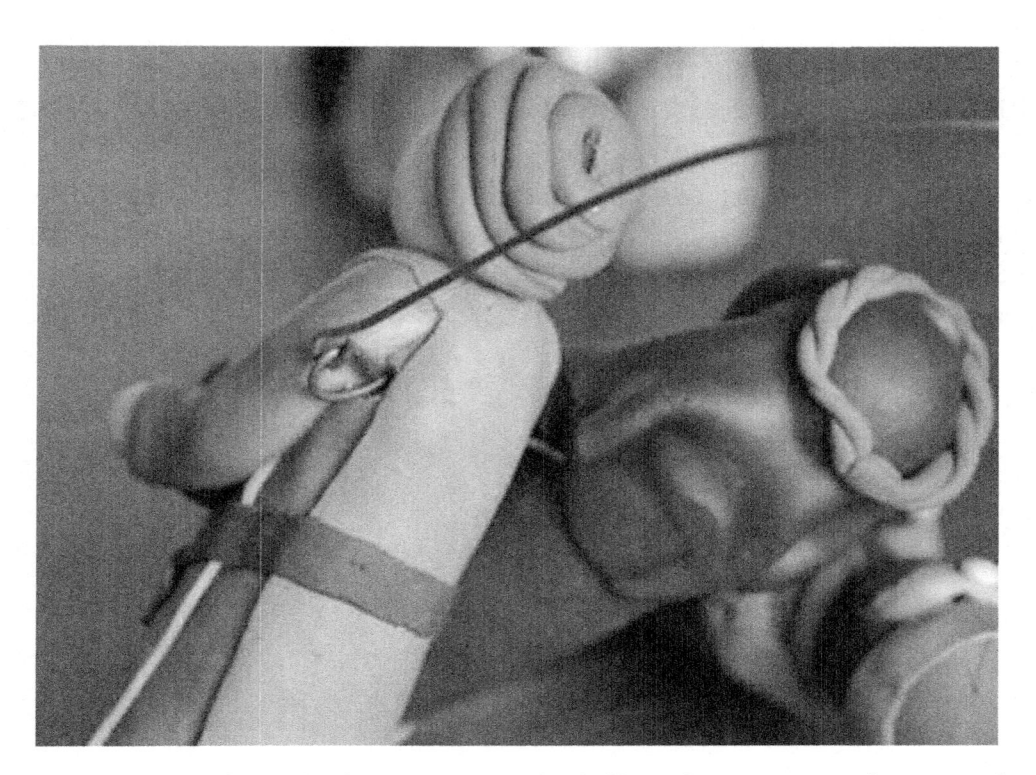

When they are done baked and cooled, line them up and run a piece of wire through the holes you made.

Close the thread by folding the ends together to make a loop, then attach another piece of thread in the same way to make a hanger.

So as the wise men are not joined by anything but the thread on which they hang, they hang freely. Instead of walking through the desert, they kind of seem to be dancing to get there. Haha! Amazing right? Surely they are.

Terrariums were all over and very common with top crafters a few years ago, but I couldn't do much of it then because one can't be into all. Here's a great learning process to help you get familiar with the terrariums concept.

A big challenge for me with this tree was how to incorporate all the different materials that you would find in the forest, without just gluing everything in a Styrofoam ball. I did some of those things, but for a tree to be interesting, you need everything the same or a lot of contrast. I had thoughts on how I can use dirt or probably using stones? In a way that would be really beautiful.

Then I saw these giant glass ornaments at my local craft shop and given a trial was next that came to me. It is probably 5 "wide, giving you an opening of about 1 inch, which is big enough to push things through.

Step 1: Begin by pushing a pile of dirt through the hole until it is about 1/4 full. I used potting soil that I had in my shed.

Step 2: Now, we need to address the difference between doing this in an ornament and doing it in a large glass jar that will never move from your counter. If you tried to keep this up during the year, all the dirt would slide back and you would be left with a big hectic mess.

Step 3: I took a little white glue and watered it until it was easy to squirt and easy for the dirt to absorb. Then squirt, taking care to catch the edges, but taking care to avoid the glass. It will dry clear, but you will still see a stain on the glass.

Step 4: Then I added a few different types of moss and spread glue everywhere as well.

Step 5: Next put in some mixed pretty forest fragments. I know it may be a little bit complex to find something small enough to go through the glass opening, so search for items that can simply be cut apart. I proceeded to the section of the craft shop that carried floral picks for wreaths. There was a lot of good stuff to pick from, and on a very smaller scale that the stuff in the rest of the floral department. I just threw in some clippings off a faux pine branch, a few fake berries, and a glittery plastic branch of something or other.

This Terrarium ornaments will be heavier than average, so ensure you pick a sturdy place it. I also go for wire ornament hooks rather than my usual fishing line. The wire enables it easier to hold firmly.

CHAPTER 12: PROJECT IDEAS TO MAKE MONEY

We begin from introduction down to standalone practical projects. Going on to learning how to make quilled flowers to creating fantastic quilled patterns, check out these selected quilling projects ideas for beginners. There are all varieties of items you can craft on your own, though they often look more difficult to make than they actually are when you start.

QUILLING SCROLLS

Similar to heart designs, you can shape the ends of a folded quilling strip so that they curve outward. I used this scrolling technique to create stems and leaves on this floral card. The flower heads were formed around a small loose circle with ribbons of feather strips.

QUILLING NECKLACES AND EARRINGS

In addition to using feathers on cards, you can also make some fantastic feather jewelry, like this feather necklace. Start by cutting a shape out of cardboard and wrapping a strip of quilling paper several times around the outside. Make a variety of small loose circles in various colors to fit inside the shape, then add 3D glitter on the top to seal.

QUILLING A, B, C

After mastering some forms of quilling, why not combine them to create a framed decorative design? From abstract patterns to intricate wildlife and fairytale designs, let your imagination run wild. Draw the chosen letter and carefully glue the edge of the feather strips around it. Surround the letter with your choice of quilled shapes to create this colorful decor.

QUILLING GREETING

Start quilling greetings using the scroll method. Write your feeling in pencil, first, then cut strips of quilling paper, wrap the ends, and glue along the edges.

QUILLING VASES

QUILLING HEARTS

CONTEMPORARY QUILLED ANGEL

Children and adults can also make this modern feather angel in less than 15 minutes. Can you imagine an entire Christmas tree adorned with these angels from top to bottom? It is certainly possible because they are very easy to do. You can create quickly enough for your entire "Angel Tree" in a few hours. Your kids will love participating in this Christmas craft. Who knows - maybe this will become an annual holiday tradition for your family.

QUILLED FLOWER PENDANT

Paper quilling naturally lends itself to jewelry projects. This beautiful pendant is made of pink and blue eyes around a circular spiral. Paste a pearl and you're done. The girls will love this project.

BRIGHTLY COLORED CHRISTMAS VILLAGE CRAFT

Craft a modern paper tale of a Christmas village. You don't need to have an artistic bone in your body to get good results on this craft project. The Vila de Natal paper is particularly easy to create because it can be printed. What you need to download from the web, print, and cut. Creating something spectacular is not easier!

The village looks great as it is, but you can take it to the next level by adding a few light bulbs to turn the houses into light fixtures. This is an excellent craft for those who want to add a homey touch to their holiday decor, but have little time during the busy holiday season.

RED AND WHITE CHRISTMAS ADVENT CALENDAR

This Christmas advent calendar craft project is charming, fun, and unique! Fill the small boxes of kraft paper with small treasures suitable for the recipient, then decorate them with red and white decorative items. Watch your children's eyes shine every day as they discover small toys or candies in the boxes. What a fun way to count the days until Christmas.

CHRISTMAS SHADOW BOX

Advanced paper craftsmen will love making this shadow box for Christmas scenes. You will be happy to know that everything in the scene, including the painting, is made of paper. Although this shadowbox takes some time and skill to make, the results are worth it. You will have an impressive Christmas decoration that adds the Christmas spirit and ambiance to your home decor.

Printed in Great Britain
by Amazon

54154738R00071